Hesiod's Calendar

ROBERT SAXTON was born in Nottingham in 1952 and now lives in north London, where he is the editorial director of an illustrated book publishing company. His first collection of poetry, *The Promise Clinic*, was published by Enitharmon Press in 1994. Then followed two collections from Carcanet/OxfordPoets: *Manganese* in 2003 and *Local Honey* in 2007. He is also represented in Faber's *Poetry Introduction 7* and the Carcanet/OxfordPoets anthology *Oxford Poets 2001*. In 2001 he won the Keats–Shelley Memorial Association's poetry prize for 'The Nightingale Broadcasts'. Robert Saxton's website may be visited at www.robertsaxton.co.uk.

T0096455

Also by Robert Saxton from Carcanet Press/OxfordPoets

Manganese
Local Honey

ROBERT SAXTON

Hesiod's Calendar

A Version of Hesiod's *Theogony*
and *Works and Days*

OxfordPoets

CARCANET

First published in Great Britain in 2010 by

Carcanet Press Limited
Alliance House
Cross Street
Manchester M2 7AQ

A CIP catalogue record for this book is available from the British Library
ISBN 978 1 90618 803 0

The publisher acknowledges financial assistance from Arts Council England

Typeset by XL Publishing Services, Tiverton
Printed and bound in England by SRP Ltd, Exeter

for Peggy

Acknowledgements

I am overwhelmingly indebted to two editions of Hesiod in English translation: Dorothea Wender, *Hesiod: Theogony / Works and Days; Theognis: Elegies* (Penguin Classics, 1973), and Glenn W. Most, *Hesiod: Theogony / Works and Days / Testimonia* (Loeb Classical Library series, Harvard University Press, 2006). Significant variations between my version of the *Works and Days* and the translations of Wender or Most are explained in the Notes. My *Theogony* allows more licence for itself; and so the Notes on this poem cite only the most material differences, such as omissions of genealogies and borrowings from Robert Graves (see below). Line numbers given in brackets in the Foreword, Introduction and Notes are taken from the Most edition, which includes the Greek text.

I also consulted a translation of the *Works and Days* by David W. Tandy and Walter C. Neale (University of California Press, 1996), especially useful for its glosses on the technicalities of farming. I derived incidental details (all credited in the Notes) from Robert Graves, *The Greek Myths* (Pelican, 1955, in two volumes; revised 1960; Penguin, 1992, combined edition).

Extracts from *Hesiod's Calendar* have been published in *PN Review* and *Modern Poetry in Translation* (series 3, no. 10; Big Green Issue). Thanks are due to Michael Schmidt and to David and Helen Constantine for their hospitality to the project, as editors of those magazines (and in Michael Schmidt's case as publisher of Carcanet). I'm grateful to David Constantine also for his impeccable judgement as my Carcanet/Oxford*Poets* editor: his questions on my Introduction and Notes, as well as here and there on the poems themselves, have rescued me from various pitfalls.

Note to the reader
The Foreword to this book has been written in such a way that it can serve as a self-contained introduction for readers unwilling to give their time to a longer prose preamble. The Introduction proper covers at some length such topics as Hesiod the man, the legends surrounding him, his relationship to Homer, and the subject matter and character of his two major works, followed by some autobiographical notes on the background to *Hesiod's Calendar* and my choice of the sonnet form.

Contents

Foreword

Hesiod was a farmer-poet who lived in Boeotia, in mainland Greece, around the beginning of the 7th century BC. A contemporary or near-contemporary of Homer (who lived in Asia Minor), he's best known for two works, the *Theogony* and the *Works and Days*, both written in the metre of the *Iliad* and the *Odyssey*, namely dactylic hexameter. We value the *Theogony* today as the earliest account that's come down to us from the Greeks of the mythic creation of the universe, the birth of the gods, the violence of the Titan Cronus towards his father the sky god Uranus, the war between the Titans and Olympians, and the subsequent establishment by Zeus of divine (Olympian) supremacy and of an ethical framework for humankind. The *Works and Days* is admired for its literary qualities – it's a more shapely poem than the *Theogony* and shows a better control of its effects. But it's also prized for its telling of the myths of Pandora and the successive Ages of Mankind and for the insights it gives us into the daily life of ancient Greece, particularly work and survival in the countryside. Addressed to a good-for-nothing brother named Perses, it's full of worldly-wise grumbles and very precise practical and moral advice – on everything from how to cut timber for a plough to behaviour best avoided at a holy banquet (such as leaving the ladle in the mixing-bowl after helping yourself to wine).

Hesiod's Calendar attempts, in two sonnet sequences, to convert the heart of the *Theogony* and the whole of the *Works and Days* into English poetry for the modern reader. I have no Greek, and have worked from two translations of both poems into English: one in iambic pentameter by Dorothea Wender, published as a Penguin Classic; and a literal prose version by Glenn W. Most in the Loeb Classical Library series. I've made more extensive use of the Loeb than of the Penguin.

My rendering of the *Theogony* is extremely partial – only 210 lines, compared with the 1019 lines of the original. My aim for the project was to write a poetic treatment, using Hesiod as sole source, of the Greek myth of the warring clans of gods, ending with the placement at Delphi of the stone which Cronus chose to swallow, believing it was his new-born son Zeus, who it was prophesied would usurp him. The castration by Cronus of Uranus is the most dramatic episode in the narrative, and it's followed by what must be one of the most brilliant transformations in pre-modern literature, unthinkably gruesome yet ultimately redemptive: the storm-driven sea voyage of Uranus' severed genitals to Cyprus and the consequent emergence of the goddess Aphrodite from their tent of foam (like 'cuckoo spit', I can't help thinking). Concentrating on pure gold (as I saw it), I felt no loyalty to the untransmuted ore – including various name-clotted genealogies, and much else that failed to engage my interest.

My *Works and Days* is much more faithful, in its own irresponsible way, to the content of the original poem. It runs at 910 lines, compared with Hesiod's 828, the difference being accounted for by many passages I've amplified slightly to round off the meaning or elaborate an image, or to ensure that each sonnet is acceptably self-contained. My purpose was to experience Hesiod's poem at the same time (literally) as rendering the whole of it in as lively and readable a fashion as I could, and in a coherent voice neither too grave nor too light (I was keen to avoid anything as blatantly detached as Byron's 'Hail Muse! et cetera', from *Don Juan*, while being unable to resist the occasional irony). When I say I wanted to *experience* the poem, what I mean is that I rendered it blind: I read it in the process of my rendition, passage by passage, sonnet by sonnet, and not before – for the sake of freshness. The risk, which of course became sharper the more I wrote, was that I would come across something 'untranslatable' in rhyme and be forced to give up. I offer thanks to the great god Zeus, who orders our lives and commands our reverence, that I made it to the end.

Introduction

To the historian Hesiod is a shadowy figure, like Homer. But if most readers feel they know Hesiod better than Homer, that's because in the *Works and Days* he presents himself as a rounded personality – practical, god-fearing, earnest, opinionated, hard-working, thrifty, plain-speaking, burdened by the effort of making a living and by the iniquities of the ungodly. It's been said that Hesiod is the first recognisable character in Western literature. We believe in him as a human being, living and breathing just behind the veil of the text, and for this reason it's hard to imagine that the *Works and Days* was originally composed and delivered orally, as some scholars believe. The poem has the flavour of intimacy and reflection that usually comes out of a writer's relationship with an imagined readership – though that isn't necessarily to say that there aren't oral precedents.

It's in the *Theogony*, however, that Hesiod gives us that starting-point for all biographical understanding: his name. The poem begins with a 115-line passage describing and then invoking the Heliconian Muses. My version reduces this to a single introductory sonnet, for I was impatient to plunge into the action, beginning with the cosmic upheavals that set the scene for epic conflict among the gods. Actually, the Invocation, as I've called it, was the last thing I wrote. I'd finished my *Theogony* and my *Works and Days* and they amounted to seventy-nine sonnets in all: fourteen (which seemed appropriate to a sonnet sequence) plus sixty-five. The feeling that eighty would be a neater total prompted me to reconsider my initial decision to skip the *Theogony*'s preamble. I'm pleased I acted on this afterthought because in retrospect I can see the importance of Hesiod's description of his encounter with the Muses. He's tending lambs on the slopes of Mount Helicon when the daughters of Zeus come to him with the gift of a staff of laurel and then breathe a divine voice into him and command him to glorify past and future and sing of the blessed 'who always are' – but of themselves first and last. I chose to begin with the familiar formula, 'Hail...', which in the Greek is delayed till line 104. Before that the third person is used for both Muses and poet – 'One day they taught Hesiod beautiful song...' – which is how in the original version, but not in mine, the name comes to be revealed.

This name has been subjected to analysis by modern scholars.

Etymologically it appears to derive from two roots meaning 'to enjoy' and 'road'. Enjoyment is an emotion somewhat foreign to Hesiod's character but that's no reason to believe he was not so named as a baby, perhaps in the hope that the name would be self-fulfilling. His parents may have imagined him as a voyager, like his father – for if the *Works and Days* offers fact rather than fiction, Hesiod was the son of a seafaring trader who lived for a time in Cyme in Aeolis (north-west Anatolia) and after taking to the seas to escape poverty settled in the village of Ascra, near Thespiae in Boeotia, in the foothills of Mount Helicon. Or perhaps he named himself afresh, thinking of the poet's 'journey', to use the modern cliché, as one that offers a reasonable chance of self-fulfilment. Glen W. Most points out, however, that the name Hesiod sounds rather like a phrase used of the Muses four times in the preamble or proem to the *Theogony*, meaning 'sending forth their voice', and it's possible that these references show the poet spinning around his given name a fanciful pseudo-etymology that suited his new calling.

Two further aspects of Hesiod's circumstances can be gleaned from the *Works and Days*. First, the poem is addressed to his lazy, duplicitous brother, Perses, with whom the poet is embroiled in a legal dispute over their inheritance. This reprobate, who has bribed a crooked magistrate to secure a more generous settlement for himself, is exhorted to abandon idleness and greed and follow the true path of hard graft and righteousness as the gods, and particularly Zeus, prescribe.

Commentators have pointed out some discrepancies here, and it's true that a stable view of the brother's situation does not quite emerge: has dishonesty made him well-off or has laziness made him poor? Actually, I find nothing troubling about this inexactitude: it seems all of a piece with the realism of Hesiod's rambling voice, like a letter in which he's pouring out his advice and feelings whilst darting freely back and forth in time. However, some critics have been niggled by these apparent inconsistencies, concluding that Perses could perhaps be a literary device – a prism through which to focus the twin themes of work and justice. I suppose he might be, but by the same token, given the absence of reliable evidence, you could say the same about Hesiod himself – and that way headaches lie. Was he really a farmer, with a son and slaves, a plot of land and an urgent wish to keep starvation at bay? Or was he writing in an artificial style of pastoral, like Virgil in the *Eclogues* or Edmund

Spenser in the *Shepheardes Calender*? Nothing I've read supports this latter possibility: there was no literary genre of this kind, though there might well have been an oral genre – if so, Hesiod conjured from its conventions an astonishing verisimilitude.

One other significant biographical detail in the *Works and Days* is Hesiod's reference to sailing from Aulis to Chalcis, across a narrow strait, to take part in a singing competition at the funeral games of Amphidamas. Hesiod wins the prize – a brazen tripod (with a cauldron on top, in the traditional design). Some commentators in antiquity who sought to establish a clear relationship between Homer and Hesiod read this passage as a reference to the two poets pitching their skills against each other, an interpretation possibly encouraged by Hesiod's passing mention of Troy at this point and by a faint hint of the epic style.

The geographer Pausanias (2nd century AD) believed that Homer came four centuries earlier, whereas others claimed priority for Hesiod, but none of the arguments either way is wholly compelling. For example, from the 5th century BC onwards some spoke of the greatest Greek poets as a famous quartet, 'Orpheus, Musaeus, Hesiod and Homer', and commentators believed that a list like this would naturally be in chronological order. In later centuries it was sometimes felt that Hesiod's self-disclosing persona represented an evolutionary step or two beyond the anonymous martial epic, making Homer's seniority more probable. The lack of consensus seems to have facilitated a legend of contemporary rivalry, which took literary form in the 4th century BC in the summary by Alcidamas of a fabled poetic *agon*. His *Contest of Homer and Hesiod* describes the poets performing with equal skill, with the result that no clear verdict can be given. Hesiod then starts to test Homer's wisdom and experience in a series of questions ranging from 'What is best for mortal man?' to 'How many Achaeans went to Ilium with the sons of Atreus?' Homer acquits himself well in this extemporised coda to the competition and the audience applauds him vigorously and calls for him to be declared the winner. But the king gives the crown to Hesiod on the grounds that he urges men to embrace peace and husbandry, a theme far superior to war and slaughter as described by Homer. Pausanias mentions this contest too and informs us that the tripod won by Hesiod is still pointed out to tourists, in what sounds like a kind of tripod park on Helicon.

The historian Thucydides (4th century BC) was the first to tell us what happened to Hesiod shortly afterwards. Warned by an oracle that he'd die in Nemea, he fled the place without delay; but then at Oenoe in Locris he was murdered at a temple dedicated to the Nemean Zeus (proving the prophecy technically correct after all) by the sons of a man named Phegeus in revenge for his seduction of their sister (the lyric poet Stesichorus was said to have been the fruit of this union). The body was tossed into the ocean but three days later dolphins carried it back to the shore where it received a proper burial. His killers escaped by putting out to sea but their ship was caught in a storm and they perished. According to an earlier tradition (7th century BC) Hesiod's remains were disinterred by the command of the Delphic oracle and removed to an honoured spot in the marketplace of Orchomenus, a town in Boeotia where the villagers of Ascra had resettled after their homes had been sacked by the Thespians. An epitaph there declared that Hesiod's glory was supreme among men revered for their wisdom.

A vivid comparison attributed to Simonides (6th–5th century BC) suggests that Hesiod was a gardener, Homer a weaver of garlands. Planting a mythic narrative of the gods which the *Iliad* and the *Odyssey* harvested to create a divine framework for these two epic sagas, the *Theogony* is one of our most important sources of classical myth. The action begins with a Big Bang – an explosive storm of cosmic and divine energies. Adding to our impression of a whirlpool of interacting forces, Hesiod moves freely between different modes of being, mingling the geophysical (Earth, Night, Sky and so on) with the supernatural (gods, goddesses, nymphs). Time appears jumbled too: 'wooded mountains' emerge even before the basic tectonics of land and sea are settled. Two human emotions stir the primal brew: lust and hatred. Monsters are born, differing from the gods only in being deformed and lacking supernatural authority – though they might well be terrifically strong. Out of this elemental drama a clear narrative of dynastic succession develops, with two distinct episodes of filial violence – Cronus' castration and usurpation of his father, the sky god Uranus; and the supplanting of Cronus and his Titan army by Zeus, his last-born, to establish the Olympian order of gods (so called from their headquarters on Mount Olympus). It was Zeus who was to provide throughout Greece the framework of values by which Hesiod's contemporaries were required to live.

Before I began my version of the *Theogony* I was already familiar with this mythic narrative, though not with its source text in Hesiod. I'd been involved with the story professionally as the editor of various accounts written by academics for a popular readership. One morning, commuting by Tube to my job in London's West End, for no particular reason I read a short booklet on 'The Origins of the Gods' issued with my *Guardian* newspaper the previous Saturday (12 January 2008) – it was the first of a series on Greek myths, retold by James Davidson. Editors experience a constant cycle of learning and forgetting. I knew the approximate outline of the myth of the Titans and Olympians but I'd forgotten many of the details, and I'm not sure I knew until then the fate of the stone the Titan Cronus is duped into swallowing. Mindful of a prophecy that one of his own sons will overthrow him, Cronus goes to his partner Rhea (his sister) each time she gives birth, seizes the baby from her lap and pops it down his gullet. The *Guardian* booklet reminded me that Rhea gives birth to one child, Zeus, in secret and hides him in a cave on Crete, carrying him through the night wrapped in blankets. When Cronus demands the baby she hands him in its place a stone, similarly swaddled. Cronus gulps this bundle down, thinking he's successfully dealt with yet another potential usurper. Zeus grows to maturity within a year. He vanquishes Cronus in a wrestling match at Olympia, the first of the Olympic games. Then Zeus frees the one-eyed Cyclopes from their captivity (imposed by Uranus, Cronus' father) in a secret hiding place in Earth (Cronus' mother), and in gratitude they give him thunderbolts and lightning – powerful weapons they alone know how to make. Zeus forces his father to regurgitate his 'wicked dinners'. First to emerge is what he most recently swallowed: the stone. Zeus has this set up at Delphi – a memorial to the start of his reign as supreme Olympian deity. Then one by one Zeus' brothers and sisters emerge from Cronus' belly, 'glad to see once more the light of day'.

It was January and I was eager to make a start on my first poem of the year. The myth of the Titans and Olympians seemed a promising subject. I was drawn in particular by the weirdness of the castration myth and the way in which a grotesque act of violence unexpectedly flowers in beauty with the birth of Aphrodite; also, by the strangeness of the stone-swallowing and the subsequent disgorging of the Olympians in reverse order of their disappearance. The commemorative siting of the stone had the makings of a satisfying ending. Knowing that Hesiod was the principal source for the myth, I bought Dorothea Wender's Penguin Classics edition, which also includes the *Works and Days*. I decided, for reasons I'll explain later, to tackle the poem as a sonnet sequence. My idea was to focus on just the basic outline of the dynastic myth of Cronus and Zeus, using Hesiod to supply the details.

In her introduction Wender makes no bones about her frustration with the *Theogony*. Promising subject matter, in her opinion, is often treated too hastily, while dull topics are excessively padded out; too many lines are devoted to names; too much of the action is bafflingly imprecise. Dramatic climaxes are spoilt by repetitious hyperbole. 'Homer gets more excitement out of a footrace,' she writes, 'than Hesiod does out of a full-scale war in heaven.' I agree that the *Theogony* is not an enthralling read. Scanning the poem as a whole did nothing to encourage me to broaden my scope. I was never tempted to include, for example, the detailed iteration of the Titans' progeny (lines 211–616: I squeeze this into an octave) nor the final battle of Zeus against Earth's last offspring, Typhoeus (820–80: I ignore this altogether). Even the story of Prometheus, punished by Zeus for stealing fire for humankind and teaching people to give the gods short measure when offering them their portion of an ox, failed to inspire me – there was something half-digested about Hesiod's version and it would have been hard in any case to work the material into my scheme. (I did, however, transplant a few details of the Prometheus passage into the tale of Pandora in my *Works and Days*; IV, 4–14.)

I also skipped much of the material in the last 140 lines of the *Theogony*. Zeus takes Metis as his first wife, and just as she is about to give birth to their daughter Athena he implants her into his belly, thereby absorbing the goddess's wisdom. Then he marries Themis, who gives birth to the Horae, or Seasons (Eunomia, or Lawfulness; Dike, or Justice, a key theme of the *Works and Days*; and Eirene, or Peace), and the Fates (Clotho, Atropos and Lachesis). By Eurynome he fathers the Graces (Aglaia, Euphrosyne and Thalia); by Demeter, Persephone; by Mnemosyne, the Muses; by Leto he fathers Apollo and Artemis; by Hera he fathers Hebe, Ares and Eileithyia. He himself gives birth to Athena, who springs from his head. Further couplings follow, of Zeus and his offspring. I reduced all this fevered activity to a few lines of offhand generalisation. Then, following my original intention, I finished with the commemorative stone, at the site we now call Delphi.

Hesiod mentions the erection of the stone earlier, immediately after describing its regurgitation (497–500). Zeus, he writes, sets it in the 'broad-pathed' earth in 'holy Pytho' in a valley or cleft beneath Parnassus, as a sign for men to marvel at in days to come – Pytho being the site of the Delphic oracle. Pausanias was to claim that the stone was still there in his day, beside the tomb of Neoptolemus, son of Achilles. He writes that it was constantly anointed with olive oil and draped with strands of unwoven wool that served as offerings during religious festivals.

Having completed my *Theogony* I was hungry for more. I decided to see what would happen if I started rendering the *Works and Days* into sonnets too. Part-way through the *Theogony* I'd switched largely to the Loeb edition – I'd started with the Wender, which was easier to come by. The Loeb was certainly more appropriate as the principal source for the new venture, given that my idea this time was to render an entire poem with a fair degree of faithfulness: Wender's iambic pentameter would have exerted an unwanted pressure on my own. The prose version of Glen W. Most was also, of course, less obviously interpretative.

A close preparatory reading of the whole of the *Works and Days* might have dampened my enthusiasm by making the challenge seem more burdensome. However, after finishing the first few sonnets I did glance over the rest of the Loeb translation to see if any obvious obstacles lay in wait. There were two, as far as I could foresee. First was a set of instructions about how to make a cart (423*ff*): 'cut a mortar three feet long, and a pestle three cubits long, and an axle seven feet long... If you cut a length eight feet long, you could cut a mallet-head from it too. Cut a three-span broad wheel for a ten-palm sized cart.' Most poets would agree that it's difficult to fit measurements into a rhyme scheme. Even more daunting was the long concluding sequence on lucky and unlucky days (765–828): 'These are the days that come from counsellor Zeus: to begin with, the first, the fourth, and the seventh, a holy day... and the eighth and the ninth. Two days of the waxing month are outstanding for toiling at a mortal's works, the eleventh and the twelfth.' The worst outcome I could imagine, apart from giving up before the end for any of a whole host of possible reasons, was dropping the cart and/or the auspicious days entirely: the resulting version might still have poetic value but it would not be a version of Hesiod's *Works and Days*, any more than my fifteen-sonnet sequence on the castration of Uranus and the dethronement of Cronus is, truly, a version of Hesiod's *Theogony*. As it turned out, no such omissions were necessary.

One encouraging stroke of good fortune right at the outset was the length of the invocation to the Muses that begins the *Works and Days*: at ten lines it lends itself well to sonnet form (for unless there are disposable details, ten lines of prose will often yield about thirteen or fourteen lines when reinterpreted in rhyming verse). The passages on the successive Ages of Mankind are also convenient in this respect, with line counts of eighteen (gold), sixteen (silver), thirteen (bronze), eighteen (the demigods) and twenty-eight, or fourteen plus fourteen (iron) – a little pruning of *descriptive* detail is usually not too difficult. After this myth of the Ages, which was influential in subsequent centuries, comes the first allegorical fable in classical literature, the tale of the hawk and the nightingale; and at eleven lines this passage is also a lucky break for any sonneteer.

The first mythical episode in the poem occurs *before* the Ages. This is the story of Pandora, who is visited upon mankind as punishment for the wickedness of Prometheus. Opening the storage jar where countless miseries are kept in harmless confinement, she releases them into the world, which is henceforth blighted by sickness and toil; only Hope is left inside. Between them the stories of Pandora, the Ages, and the hawk and nightingale account for 171 of the first 212 lines of the poem. Arguably, all this narrative early on provides a link to the world of the *Theogony* – a mythic transition before the poem settles down to focus steadily on life in rural Boeotia. Another, broader connection between the two poems is the important theme of the supremacy of Zeus. In the *Theogony* Hesiod explains how this authority arose in his account of the god's ancestry and struggle for power; and then in the *Works and Days* he emphasises its implications for humanity through a miscellany of instructions, prohibitions and advice. In Zeus two thematic strands of the poem meet, for the ethical framework he imposes on mankind, requiring obedience, propriety and *work*, is an aspect of his divine *justice*.

In the introduction to her edition Dorothea Wender describes the *Works and Days* as a satisfying work of literature – a good poem. I agree with her. Some readers are bothered by the uncertainties about Perses; others by the way in which the focus shifts randomly between one theme and another; others still by the superstitious catalogue of days, thought by some to be another writer's work. If you feel, as you read my version, that the poem does have a certain coherence, you're entitled to suspect that this is because I've adopted a voice for Hesiod that is not consistently present in the original – or perhaps not present at all. I believe I could mount a spirited rebuttal of this charge, but if the question is of interest it's probably better that you come to your own conclusions, by making comparisons – perhaps starting with the literal prose translations selectively quoted on pp. 89–92 of this book.

The description in the *Works and Days* of the month of Lenaeon (late January and early February) is justly famous – though it's sometimes thought to bear the hallmark of a more sophisticated poet than Hesiod. We read of wild animals tucking their tails under their genitals, an old man curved in the wind like a wheel, a soft-skinned girl who bathes, anoints herself in oil and lies down in an innermost recess of the house. Then what really astonishes, because no less intimate in the way the scene is visualised, is the sudden switch to an alien world, inhabited by the 'boneless one' – the octopus – ravenously gnawing on its own tentacles in the icy wastes of the ocean. Other notable examples of closely observed nature, encountered from time to time among the poem's instructions on farming, are the spiders quivering in their webs in the grain storage bins before the annual sweep-out, the rain reaching up to the level of an ox's hoofprints, the cicada in its tree singing ceaselessly from beneath its wings.

Glimpses of this kind have an almost lyrical charm that contrasts attractively with the overall plainness of the poem. The predominant mode is well-argued conversational directness, driven by a strong sense of propriety that readily expresses itself in advice, admonition, distaste and praise, according to circumstances. References to the characteristic paraphernalia of rural life and to commonplace actions, such as borrowing tools from a neighbour or taming an obstreperous dog or storing sailcloth in the roof-space of a house, build up to make a lively and detailed portrait of a society. Impressions of life in Boeotia more than two and a half thousand years ago are conveyed with wonderful immediacy.

Imperatives are frequent, for Hesiod's intention is unambiguously didactic. This emphasis on instruction – moral, religious, agricultural, maritime – places the poem firmly in the genre of 'wisdom literature', which has few exponents in Greek (Theognis,

Phocylides) but numerous examples in Sumerian, Akkadian, Egyptian, Aramaic and Hebrew. The consensus seems to be that nowhere in this genre is there anything as ambitious in its scope, as well-planned in its architecture or as fully realised in its presentation of social settings and situations as the *Works and Days*.

I have not yet addressed the question of why I chose the sonnet sequence as my medium for *Hesiod's Calendar*, given that the original poems are unstanzaic and unrhyming. In the year and a half before I started my *Theogony* I'd written about twenty sonnets, as part of a conscious effort to accumulate a book of poetry (not complete at the time of writing) in which the form would feature prominently. The sonnet had entered my bloodstream and was my intuitive choice for the *Theogony*. I was interested to see what would happen if I kitted out the form in work clothes and set it to the task of storytelling. I felt in my bones that it would prove satisfyingly resilient if recruited to a job beneath its station – liberated from its more familiar role as a closet for introspection or as a locket for love. Between the flow of the language and the constraints of the formal structure I hoped to set up an engaging counterpoint – in parallel to the tension I envisaged between the conversational and the mythic. After writing two or three sonnets I found that my experiment was working sufficiently well for me to continue. The sonnet was giving an inflection to the narrative line, preventing it from becoming monotonously propulsive (there are other ways to avoid monotony, of course, but this one struck me as relatively easy and reliable); and it was doing so without drawing too much attention to itself, as a more elaborate verse form might. By the time I'd finished my *Theogony* I was convinced that my chosen medium would be suitable for the larger enterprise of converting the whole of the *Works and Days* into English poetry. If the sonnet sequence could cope with narrative, it could cope with extended disquisition, and also with a mixture of the two – indeed, perhaps it would be the optimum vehicle for such a hybrid.

In attempting to render Hesiod in a run of sonnets I discovered early on the importance of being relaxed about the *volta*, or 'turn' – the division between octave and sestet that traditionally marks a break or hinge in the argument. Arranging a narrative around a succession of turns would have a unifying and therefore deadening effect on the rhythm of events. Moreover, any attempt to produce anything like a translation, or quasi-translation, would be severely hampered by such a formal constraint: it would be necessary to cut or add material to keep the octave-sestet division intact. (I *have* added in my *Works and Days* but not to the extent that consistently preserving the *volta* would have required.)

In my opinion, to ignore the *volta* in a sonnet, and sometimes indeed to enjamb across it, is rather like choosing not to avail oneself of all the capabilities of a software program – that is to say, it's a valid use of the 'technology'. In the event, I was able to retain some kind of decisive pause, shift or contrast after the octave, or at least end a sentence there, with considerable frequency – in ten out of the fifteen sonnets in the *Theogony* and thirty-four out of the sixty-five in the *Works and Days*. It's far-fetched, I know, but I can't help thinking of these meetings of form and sense as being rather like those moments in a sitar or sarod recital when the instrumentalist and the tabla player finish a passage simultaneously on the same resounding beat.

For the sonnets in my *Theogony* I used a compound rhyme scheme: the Shakespearean octave (*abab cdcd*) followed by the Petrarchan sestet (*efg efg*). In the *Works and Days*, however, I opted for *abba cddc* in the octave, as I believe it's more elegant and also has the practical advantage, I sometimes (hesitantly) think, of lending itself to a clear working method: you get the couplet right first, then tinker to perfect the enclosing rhyme – whereas *abab cdcd* offers no obvious order of priorities.

But I find myself now in territory far from Hesiod – among the technicalities of writing formal poetry in English. Of course, there's more I could say about this and other aspects of *Hesiod's Calendar* – for example, the whole question of diction, which is fundamental to the imagined viewpoint of the *Theogony* and to the personalised voice of the *Works and Days*. I could talk about wit and sincerity, playfulness and respect, anachronism and fidelity, mischief and decorum. However, I must resist the temptation to linger in this solipsistic Aegean of the poetic imagination. The time is long overdue to weigh anchor and set sail for the mainland – before Zeus loses his patience with me altogether and Poseidon brings wrathful storms upon my head.

Theogony

Invocation

Hail, lovely gracious Muses, who dance round
the altar of your father Zeus and sing
his glory. Once when I was pasturing
lambs on the slopes of Helicon, on holy ground

above my valley, in a vision you came to me
and handed me a laurel staff, and blew
into my larynx and my soul the true
poetic gift, and sealed my destiny:

to glorify the great god Zeus, and tell
of what is past and what is yet to be,
praising him and all his offspring in a burst

of reverent song and weaving a heavenly spell
round heavenly deeds to cure men's misery.
Let's start with creation. Show me. What came first?

I

Chaos was first: no dream, no fear, no rain,
only an idiot swirl in a cosmic brew,
till Chaos scratched a planet from its brain,
which yearned, of course, as bodies always do.

This was broad-shouldered Earth, also named Gaia,
base-camp of the gods who from the peak
of Mount Olympus – there being no peak higher –
watch over us as we squabble, squirm and squeak.

On the same day the Abyss was quarried: Tartarus,
into which an anvil took nine days to fall,
convenient oubliette for living scraps.

And Love was let loose too: Eros, a fuss
of chemicals felt by gods and men in thrall
to a maddening itch – doomed from the start perhaps.

II

Night too was a child of Chaos. Another
was the Underworld, Erebos, with whom Night lay,
attracted by her deep, dark, handsome brother.
And from this union Night gave birth to Day –

and Space, or Aether, the upper atmosphere,
more subtle than the air men breathe below.
Earth bore the sky god Uranus to cover her,
and fill her lakes and make her rivers flow.

Then she gave birth to long and lovely hills
where Nymphs could dwell in secret fern-clad caves
and let themselves be glimpsed, and sometimes more,

and Love might rest, gloating on all her kills.
Then without dalliance Earth spawned the swollen waves
of the barren sea, Pontus: her cuspidor.

III

And then Earth coupled with Uranus: it was bound
to happen. A shower of sperm like spring rain
fell on the hills and hollows, pooling on the ground
and soaking in. Earth became pregnant again.

Her fertility was prodigious: out
came the twelve Titans, born to be overthrown –
the first being Oceanus, who girdled her about
with a river, silver setting for the blue-green stone.

He and his siblings were not gods exactly,
more like divine giants. Here's the complete list:
Coeus came next, then Crius, Iepatus, Hyperion,

Theia, Rhea, Themis, Mnemosyne,
lovely Thetys (in other words, much-kissed),
Phoebe, and lastly Cronus, the malevolent one.

IV

Earth also had some even stranger progeny
by Uranus: a rabble of monstrous anthropods.
Among them were the terrifying Cyclopes, three
one-eyed simpletons, even less like proper gods

than their Titan kinsfolk. Brontes, Steropes
and Arges were their names. They had tattooed faces.
They were skilled at forging swords, uprooting trees
and building walls – hardly the Three Graces.

As we shall see, these were the ones who found
the thunder and the lightning-bolt and gave
them to Zeus. Three other sons, no less belligerent,

had a hundred arms and fifty heads to astound
their enemies – so easy to be brave
when thus equipped. (Their names are unimportant.)

V

Now Uranus loathed his uglier offspring
and banished them from the moment of their birth
to a secret hiding-place, pitch-black and stifling…
where better than the bowels of Mother Earth?

Savouring this wickedness, he dribbled, crazy-eyed.
Earth, in mourning, felt her belly stretch and strain,
punched by windmilling arms, a brawl inside
her making her nauseous, dizzy with pain.

Grief-stricken for her children, angry, she hatched a plan.
Quarrying from herself a mineral, 'adamant',
invincibly hard, she fashioned a mighty sickle.

Then she addressed her Titans: 'You must unman
your evil father. I'm sick of this heartless torment.
I thirst for revenge – don't tell me you're fickle!'

VI

Hearing these words, the Titans, filled with alarm,
fell silent for a minute. Then, tremblingly,
Cronus, who'd always wished his father harm,
spoke out: 'Dear Mother, you can rely on me.

I've hated that monstrous tyrant from the start –
without him there'd be no such thing as shame.
Proudly for you I'll take the hero's part
and in a brave venture earn a hero's name.'

All this great Earth was gratified to hear.
Taking Cronus aside, she talked him through her scheme
and placed in his hands the saw-toothed scimitar.

Concealed, he waited till the sky god tiptoed near
under cover of Night to inseminate Earth's dream –
careless, as all excited lovers are.

VII

Longing for love he lay across the land,
fully extended. Cronus, spying on his lust
from behind a stone, reached out with his right hand
to grab his bush, then with his left hand thrust

the jagged blade to harvest the genitals,
which he flung behind him with a mighty throw
so they went spinning high over hills and dales.
From their wound, blood gouts fell on Earth below.

Nine months later Earth bore the Erinnyes – Furies
who avenge parricide eternally
to discourage jealous sons from gross defiance

(that this deterrent fails to work is curious).
Also from that blood sprang the Meliae –
nymphs of the ash; also, some say, the Giants.

VIII

The massive organs, landing with a splash,
rolled in the waves like a wounded whale.
White foam frothed out around the immortal flesh,
and in that tent of spittle hatched a girl.

From embryo to child to woman she grew,
impatiently, as the strange craft drifted west
to holy Cythera, till a sudden storm blew
the foamy thing to Cyprus where it came to rest.

Then out she stepped: Aphrodite. Goddess.
Irresistible, and already beloved
by Love. Wily. Vengeful. Expert in bed.

The shore was pebbly, nevertheless
flowers sprang up from her footsteps as she moved
up the beach. Doves cooed around her lovely head.

IX

An age of procreation dawned meanwhile –
fast and furious. Night gave birth to Sorrow,
Doom, Death, Sleep, Sadness, a tribe of Dreams, Guile,
the Hesperides – the apples of her eye. The morrow

was enlivened by Night's work. Many births occurred,
with various parents: monsters, nymphs, rivers,
the Blame that follows when you break your word,
a host of powers – life-takers, life-givers.

In this frenzy of love Cronus ravished
his sister Rhea, who bore him brilliant offspring:
Hestia, Demeter, golden-slippered Hera,

Hades, who from the shores of the Underworld fished
for souls, Poseidon, mighty oceanic king,
and Zeus, than whom no new-born god was dearer.

X

Now we left Uranus, the sky god, fairly
out of his mind with rage – humiliated
and in pain. 'You face a miserable destiny,'
he roared at Cronus, his rebel son. 'It's fated

one of your own children will steal your throne.'
Earth echoed this prophecy. But Cronus was keen
that of all the Titan family he alone
should hold royal rank, and so a quarantine

must be imposed on any child of his.
As his mistress came to full term, once a year,
he snatched the new-born from her lap

and swallowed it. And these atrocities
by the sky god mortified the goddess Rhea:
each vile abduction hit her like a thunderclap.

XI

She went to her parents, Heaven and Earth,
and pleaded with them to devise some kind of plan,
which willingly they did. Before the birth
of Zeus, father of gods and men,

she sailed to Crete and had the baby there.
Earth wrapped it up warm, took it to a cave
in the Aegean Hill and gave it secret care.
Zeus flourished – and grew to be kingly and brave

within scarcely a year. As usual Cronus came
to Rhea and demanded the latest infant.
Obediently, she handed him a stone

swaddled in blankets. He gulped it down, the same
as all the rest; then he resumed his rant.
Rhea showed due grief, with a convincing moan.

XII

Now in the ascendant, Zeus prepared for war.
Prophetically on the night sky blazed a comet.
Earth mixed Cronus a 'potion' to restore
his nerves – in fact, a poison, which made him vomit,

sicking up first the stone he'd swallowed thinking
it was his youngest child; then one by one
the Olympians (as they came to be known), blinking
now, dazzled, confused, in the glare of the Grecian sun –

the backbone of an army, drilled by Zeus,
who to augment them freed the hundred-handed clods
from Tartarus, and with them the Cyclopes,

a ragged crew of rare strategic use
for their lethal thunder-bolts and lightning-rods.
Each giant's hundred clubs was a grove of trees.

XIII

A grim world war for ten years was pursued
with neither army sniffing the scent of victory.
But on a whim Zeus fed ambrosia, the food
of the gods, and nectar, their drink, to his motley

anthropods, who were filled with a surge of pride
in their strength and bravery, a creditable lust
for the fight. Like a gang of gods upon a bride,
they jumped on the Titans. They flung and thrust

and fired every kind of weapon and projectile.
Each hundred-hands abandoned trees for rocks,
while Zeus rampaged with lethal lightning-spears.

Woods burned, and carnage went the extra mile.
Seas boiled. Even Tartarus felt seismic shocks.
Her lakes all lost, Earth bathed in scalding tears.

XIV

The Titans were routed, clapped in massive chains
and thrown to Tartarus, where still they lie
in darkness, all around and in their brains,
eternally – even the gods can't hear them cry.

Zeus cordoned off the place with walls of bronze
and set the hundred-handed ones on guard.
Above ground, shining like a thousand suns,
he ordered their fate: this side of him was hard

as diamonds but the soft side married, thrice.
Which side coupled adulterously, prolifically,
is difficult to judge. Great gods were born,

and goddesses. One memorial will suffice:
the stone that Cronus swallowed, now at Delphi,
on an ancient hill, kissed by the sacred dawn.

Works and Days

I

Pierian Muses, lovers of song: tell
now of your father, Zeus, and sing his praise,
who buries or illuminates men's days.
This one's nobody, that one we all know well.

He bleeds the rich, makes a poor man head of state.
With ease he levels mountains, raises plains,
to the flooded brings drought, to the thirsty, rains.
He hobbles the proud and makes the crooked straight.

O thunder god, whose home is high above
on snowy Olympus, half-way to the stars,
please listen to my humble prayer to you.

Protect us with your aegis and your love.
Restore our broken laws and heal our scars.
Let my song to my brother, Perses, echo true.

II

Strife is no only child: there are two of them.
One, from those in the know, wins endless praise,
the other's blamed for blighting good men's days
with war, murder and mindless mayhem.

The cruel one we'd be foolish not to appease,
but his brother, eldest child of darkest Night,
was placed on Earth to set our bearings right.
Even lazy folk are forced down on their knees

to scrub or plant, or are shackled to the plough.
Neighbour against neighbour, eagerly we compete –
it's good for us to have to strive so hard.

This farmer's inspired by another's prize cow,
that one looks lovingly at another's wheat.
It's beggar against beggar, bard against bard.

III

O Perses, keep these words close to your heart:
Don't let bad Strife distract you from your job
and tempt you to idle politics. Shun the mob.
No one has time to lobby in the court

or dabble in public life till he has stored
up a year's supply of grain, Demeter's gift –
you've no such hope. So let's repair our rift
before one of us reaches for his sword.

We'll put our quarrel to Zeus, whose laws are just.
When we inherited our property,
you grabbed the glutton's share and took the trouble

to cultivate one of those magistrates men trust
only to take a bribe. This crook won't see
that one half can be valued more than double.

IV

The gods have hidden many things we need.
We could work for a day, if it were otherwise,
and earn enough to buy a year's supplies.
Our tools we'd sell. Luxury would be our creed.

Zeus was the one who filled our lives with toil,
as punishment. We'd tried to fool him when
an ox was apportioned between gods and men,
and Zeus was offered only bones to boil.

Prometheus had taught deception to the race
of men, so Zeus gave thought to how he might
retaliate. First he sequestered the gift of fire.

But Prometheus found a clever hiding-place
for the flame in a fennel stalk. Out of spite,
Zeus thought up a torture at one with man's desire.

V

'All men will love this ruin in their hearts,'
he said, and laughed. Then, on a doleful day,
Hephaestus, the smith god, shaped for him some clay
and gave it a pulse, a voice, a few moving parts,

a face, like a goddess's, almost divine,
the lovely figure of a virgin girl,
with lustrous hair, curl upon flowing curl,
apt to confuse men's brains, like too much wine.

Athena taught her to weave and loaned her a gown
and belt. Aphrodite blessed her with fame
for beauty, distilling for every sense a tonic.

The Seasons wove spring flowers to make her crown,
while Hermes gave her slyness and a name,
Pandora, meaning 'all gifts' – this was ironic.

VI

The trap was set. Zeus sent his messenger
Hermes with the luscious girl to Epimetheus,
dim-witted, short-sighted twin of Prometheus
who'd warned his brother of the mortal danger

to all mankind if ever he should accept
a present from Zeus. Of course, this slipped his mind
the moment he saw Pandora, who'd been designed
to muddle clearer brains. This gift he kept.

Before this time men lived a carefree life,
unaware of grief, disease or painful toil –
these existed only in a jar with the lid

screwed tight, out of harm's way. No one knew Strife,
for it was forbidden by divine royal
decree to peek inside. Pandora did.

VII

Mischief incarnate, like some devil's bride,
she scattered pains and evils among men.
Inside the jar, when someone closed it again,
Hope was trapped – a charm against suicide.

But out flew the rest like a swarm of bees,
thousands of troubles, wandering the face
of the Earth over land and sea and every place
inhabited by men, bringing them to their knees.

Diseases visit us any time of day,
then uninvited come again at night,
foot-soldiers of the strong and silent kind –

for the great god Zeus has taken away
their power of speech, to give an extra bite
to the harm they cause. We can't escape his mind.

VIII

And here's another tale you ought to know.
Once, divine and human beings were equal.
Under Cronus, gods made the men we call
the race of gold. Free of worry, sorrow

and old age, they lived on delicious wild food.
Death came to them like sleep. Every good thing
was theirs. Snake and scorpion bared no sting.
Each lived at ease, ruled only by his mood.

Happy, at peace, with every want supplied,
loved by the gods, they were blessed – but disappeared,
possibly in an earthquake or a flood.

In the wrinkled earth their spirits now reside.
Givers of wealth, and joy where music's heard,
they still have kingly rights. They are holy and good.

IX

Silver was the next race the gods made,
inferior to the gold – shorter, less clever.
To raise a child seemed to take forever:
for a hundred years the massive baby played

by its mother's side. Grown up, they lived brief,
anguished lives. Out of sheer stupidity
they couldn't stop doing each other injury;
and they forsook the gods, which brought them grief.

Their crime was lack of self-control, combined
with utter selfishness. Their chief disgrace
was neglect of sacrifice, leaving the altars bare.

Zeus, son of Cronus, was angry, and not inclined
to be lenient. He eliminated the whole race
for dishonouring the gods. Heathens, beware!

X

Then Zeus forged a third human race, from bronze,
worse than the silver dynasty – brutish, weird,
frightening. They loved violence and appeared
deaf to all but battle's shrieks and groans.

Fierce and strong, they ate no food from a farm,
only wild animals. No army could subdue
them. Their weapons were bronze, their houses too.
They killed each other in an orgy of self-harm.

Nameless, they ended up in the dark, chill
house of Hades, leaving behind no ghosts,
no tell-tale traces of themselves – not one.

Great soldiers though they'd been, Death with his will
of iron silenced their heaven-piercing boasts,
capturing from bronze the brightness of the sun.

XI

And when this race was ushered underground,
the son of Cronus put another clan
upon this Earth, who immediately began
to prove themselves more just and good around

each other. This was the race before ours,
with human mothers – the so-called demi-gods.
Some fell in battle, powerless against tall odds;
some, seeking the flocks of Oedipus, by the towers

of seven-gated Thebes gave up the ghost;
while some for Helen's sake were killed at Troy.
Of many a brighter, posthumous story

's told, of landing off life's farthest coast
on the Isles of the Blessed: eternal joy!
This race of heroes well deserve their glory.

XII

Zeus made a fifth, iron race. I'm a member
of this clan – and wish I weren't, believe me.
By day we work and grieve ceaselessly,
by night some of us fade like an ember

cooling to ash in death. The great gods deal
a mixture of bad and good. Zeus will not spare
our kind. Babies will be born with grizzled hair.
Sons will defy their fathers, guests will steal

from hosts, true friendship will be all too rare.
Men will loathe parents who grow old too soon
and cruelly evict them from the family home.

They'll let whole towns fall into disrepair.
Wretched and godless, they'll worship the moon…
or nothing. Athens will sink with the rise of Rome.

XIII

Someone who keeps his word will be thought weak
and men will lavish praise unstintingly
upon the insolent and cruel, do injury
to better men, excel in double-speak

sworn upon oath with the sincerest eyes.
Envy will roam among the unenviable.
Fleeing Earth for Olympus to escape the cull,
dressed all in white, so graceful and so wise,

will go the spirits Righteousness and Shame,
abandoning mankind to join the pantheon
of gods for their more virtuous company.

Honour burns with a bright yet faltering flame
we shield from winds unleashed where evil's done –
namely, on Earth, whose doom's our destiny.

XIV

Now here's a fable, clear as the wine-dark sea.
A hawk in the clouds flew over hill and dale,
clutching in his claws a captured nightingale
who cried out, somewhat naively, 'Pity me!'

The hawk dismissed with scorn this desperate cry:
'Stupid bird, why bother? I'm deaf to your appeal.
Your master holds you tight. Friend, this is real!
You'll go where I choose, despite your minstrelsy,

so useless now. The gods would have to agree,
I could eat you or let you go – I'm in control.
Only a fool, however well he sings,

would match himself against a force like me –
to his disgrace he'd forfeit body and soul.'
So said the hawk, flying swift on tireless wings.

XV

O Perses, be careful: you must keep Greed at bay.
It will infect a man of yeoman stock
as much as a chip off a more illustrious block.
It turns our head and leads our wits astray.

Better to follow Justice, which will win
the fight against corruption. The callow youth
will learn from experience how the god of Truth
outruns a crooked verdict. Bad men spin

the facts. Gloves off, they bludgeon Justice down
into the dirt of an alley where we hear
the cries of struggle, the shush of bribery.

But Justice, wrapped in a mist, steals back to town
and rounds up those who rule the place by fear.
She arrests the mob, setting the informant free.

XVI

When judges are fair to all, life tastes more sweet.
The city thrives, its citizens content.
Since Peace holds sway without impediment,
families prosper. Most have enough to eat.

Famine, when it does strike, comes without guilt –
it's no one's fault. Lightly men tend the land,
conjuring the good life with a skilful hand
in fields all parcelled like a patchwork quilt.

The earth provides. Oaks have acorns above
and bees below; sheep wear luxurious fleeces.
Women bring up sons, with a gentle touch,

who turn out like their fathers. Justice brings love,
joy and abundance. Misery ceases.
Few emigrate – men all love home too much.

XVII

Some toil, however, on the fields of Pride –
despicable folk. Zeus with far-seeing eye
observes them, and often a whole city
suffers for their ungodly deeds. The tide

of fortune turns, bringing famine and plague.
The people die. Women become infertile.
Villages empty, mile upon desperate mile.
Farmers lie sick in bed, doctors are vague.

Or sometimes the son of Cronus will destroy
an army, or a well, or a city wall,
or a fleet of ships at anchor in the bay.

The gods will smash such projects like a toy
if they see the need for punishment at all.
Watchful and strict, they're never far away.

XVIII

They spy on crooked judges who ride roughshod
over their fellow men and fail to exercise
good law. Some thirty thousand pairs of eyes
roam over Earth on behalf of the great god

Zeus. Tirelessly they visit every court –
immortal spirits, invisible in the mist
that cloaks them, tracking every turn and twist
of every lawsuit, every scruple bought.

One such is Justice, sweet daughter of Zeus,
the virgin every Olympian god reveres.
Whenever a criminal's wrongfully discharged,

she sobs to her father about the abuse
of the system, and he avenges all her tears.
Evil falls back on evil men, enlarged.

XIX

Zeus misses nothing we do: the god's aware
of how well run each city is. As for me,
I'm troubled by some instinct not to be
just, and by the thought that my son will fare

badly as a beacon among the benighted –
it's dangerous to be truthful in a liars' den.
But I pray, great Zeus, make me innocent again.
Return me to the fold of the perfect-sighted.

Perses, too, I beg you: don't be ill-starred.
Animals were made to tear each other's throats
out, men to follow rules – which makes more sense.

Zeus punishes all malefactors hard –
their families too. The good wear warmer coats.
Their houses thrive on their obedience.

XX

These are grave matters, brother: mark me well.
Evil lies all around. It's tragic that
she lives nearby and the road to her's so flat.
Effortlessly she weaves her binding spell.

Goodness is trickier: the gods have given us a sea
of sweat to get through and the path is steep,
long and rocky at first, though if you keep
your faith you'll find her at the summit easily.

The best of men is he who thinks things through,
who can work out what might happen and be sure
to get successful projects under way.

He who listens to good advice is worthy too.
But anyone who neither thinks nor listens before
he acts is hardly worth his weight in hay.

XXI

O Perses, my brother, listen carefully.
Work till Hunger can only *wish* you dead
and till Demeter, revered and garlanded,
loves you (as I should) and fills your granary.

Though Hunger's loyal to him who fails to strive,
gods and good men have nothing but contempt
for those who choose to think themselves exempt
from work, like useless drones in a beehive.

Work brings the world's best things within our reach
and wins from the deathless gods a radiant smile.
It's far from shameful, if the truth be known:

quite the reverse. The lazy man's a leech,
bleeding himself – his blood's just bloodless bile.
Don't envy other's wealth: accrue your own.

XXII

Don't squeeze it from others, though: better, you'll find,
to receive it as a gift from the gods – a reward
for effort. If a man gets wealthy by sword
or stealth, as often happens when the mind

is clouded by greed and Shame gives way
to Shamelessness, the gods eclipse his sun,
his household shrivels, and he learns that no one
should expect ill-gotten gains to stay

the night. Moreover, he who harms a guest
or suppliant, or sleeps with his brother's wife,
or hurts an orphan child who can't yet speak,

or attacks his ageing father before he's dressed,
such a man angers Zeus. Before his life
has run its course, he'll be sorry he was weak.

XXIII

Now, open your heart to god-pleasing ways alone.
Do your sacrifices as the gods require,
with reverence and with heaven-seeking fire,
laying juicy thigh-bones on the altar-stone.

Let incense mingle with the evening's airs,
and with the dawn's when daylight's glimpsed again.
The gods will favour you, so other men
will never buy your land, though you'll buy theirs.

Don't feast your enemy, only your friend.
Be cordial towards your neighbour, who if trouble
comes to your farm is there at hand before

your kinsman's strapped on arms – you'll tend
to hang on to your cows. Pay back double
when you borrow: his loyalty's worth far more.

XXIV

Don't profit in disreputable ways,
for any gains such practices might yield
are just as bad as losses. A contract sealed
with an honest handshake and a gracious phrase

is how you'll prosper: don't betray a friend.
When someone visits, give if they give to you;
but if not, don't. This hoary maxim's true:
it's the giver who gets the best gifts in the end.

Giving's attractive, grabbing's quite obscene –
grim donor of death. Whoever gives ungrudgingly,
however much, takes pleasure from the deed

and feels his spirit grow. But he who's mean
enough to take even a small thing, shamelessly –
his heart freezes, turning small and hard with greed.

XXV

Your household store is your foundation-stone.
It's good your wealth's at home, beneath your gaze.
Take what you need – that's fine. But a malaise
blights your spirit when you need more than you own.

Remember this: adding often to your store,
little by little, will one day make it huge.
Thus, brick by brick you'll build yourself a refuge
against Famine, fierce red-eyed carnivore.

It's best to take your fill when the storage jar
stands just opened or almost empty. Show
thrift in the middle: it's not worth saving dregs.

Pay your friend as promised, or you'll leave a scar;
with your brother, add a smile. Have a witness, though –
both trust and mistrust can hobble a man's legs.

XXVI

Don't be undone by a bottom-wiggling woman –
not if she's rootling in your granary.
This is one of a thousand shades of folly.
Be wise – for example, on the question of a son.

If you have two, you'll need more cash
and a longer life – yet two sons harm your health.
Just one on the father's farm increases wealth
and isn't such a drain. But don't be rash:

Zeus is ingenious at finding ways
to enrich a larger family. It's commonsense.
More hands, more work, more profit for your estate.

If profit's what you seek, this method pays.
Have many sons, and capitalise the expense
as a many-handed work machine. Procreate.

XXVII

The farmer's life will make your fortune grow.
Start the harvest when the Pleiades starts to rise.
Plough when the Sisters sink from autumn skies.
For forty nights these high-born girls lie low;

when the year rolls round, they swing into view again
as you work to sharpen your sickle-blade.
Wherever there's fertile land this law's obeyed –
in valley, on coastal strip, on inland plain.

To sow your seed, go naked – I'm serious.
Strip to your skin to plough, and strip to reap –
no better way to harvest Demeter's yield.

Strange though it sounds, this is no delirious
rite – it's expert practice. If you herd sheep,
be clothed; but not if your wealth's a golden field.

XXVIII

Work well: each crop will come to you in turn –
there'll be no need to beg from other men.
Perses, you're begging from me now, but when
you're abject like this, you'll begin to learn

how hard my heart is. I'll neither give nor lend
to you. Foolish brother, work! Your family
mustn't beg for food from neighbours who can't see
why they should care. They might, with a blend

of pity and contempt, give you a grain
or two of corn to keep you half-alive;
they might repeat this gesture once or twice.

But after that you'll bother them in vain.
Your words will fail. But if you strive,
as I've said before, you'll live. Here's my advice:

XXIX

First, get a house, a woman, and an ox
for ploughing. The woman has to be a slave,
not a wife – someone to toil in the fields and save
you time, and cushion you against hard knocks.

She's there to set up your house just as you need,
to spare you the shame of having to borrow
things and being refused, and the long, slow
agony of sitting idle while the crops plead

for their ripeness to be brought to the barn and stored.
Don't put off jobs if you can start right now.
If it's stormy, work indoors. Sharpen your knives

and sickles, do your accounts – you needn't be bored.
Your fields will soon be yearning for the plough.
The indolent bring ruin upon their lives.

XXX

When the sun's hot fury burns itself away
and mighty Zeus brings autumn rains to refresh
our spirits and put us at ease within our flesh,
and Sirius takes a smaller share of day,

a larger share of night as over our misery
it traces its arc, any tree you fell at this time,
shedding its leaves, no longer in its prime
of sprouting growth, is likeliest to be free

of worm-holes. This is the time to cut your wood.
Cut four and a half feet for a pestle; for a mortar, three.
Seven will make you an axle; but if you feel

you want a mallet-head as well, it's good
to have an extra foot. Carpenters agree:
for a standard ten-palm cart, cut a three-span wheel.

XXXI

Bent timber's there in abundance for the taking.
On the hills around your farm look for a suitable
log of holm-oak, and if you find one pull
it back to your yard, for holm-oak's just the thing

for a good, resilient, workmanlike plough-tree
for ploughing with oxen. Get one of Athena's men
to fix it firm in the plough-stock, and then
peg it with dowels to the yoke-pole sturdily.

It's best to have two ploughs in case one breaks.
As well as your assembled plough, have one
as a handy spare you've fashioned naturally –

an inferior stand-by. Elm or laurel makes
the soundest poles. For the stock, oak's the proven
best. Use holm-oak, as I've said, for the plough-tree.

XXXII

Acquire for yourself two nine-year-old oxen –
experienced beasts, strong, hard-working, big.
They won't fight in the furrows and smash your rig,
leaving all that work heartbreakingly undone.

Behind them you need a man or forty or so,
a trencherman perhaps, who's breakfasted well –
vigorous, fit, with lungs sound as a bell,
who'll keep each furrow straight like a tautened bow

and work unflaggingly. Another man
like him should follow scattering the seed,
not wasting any. Forty's the best age,

for sure, because a younger worker can
be tangled up with sex – the carnal greed
that makes his concentration disengage.

XXXIII

Every year when you hear the voice of cranes
calling from above, out of cloudy skies,
they're telling you to plough. They're keen to advise
you of the imminence of winter rains.

This stabs the heart of the man who has no oxen.
For now's the time you should be fattening your team
indoors. It's easy to have a wishful dream
of borrowing oxen and a cart. But then

it's easy for your neighbour to refuse
because he has no spare capacity.
A dreamer might think of building such a cart –

the fool doesn't know that a cart fit to use
has a hundred boards. He's missed his opportunity.
You have to get things ready, part by part.

XXXIV

When it's ploughing time, be tireless: plough away,
you and your slaves, whether it's dry or wet,
all season long. Start early. If you get
to your fields at dawn, and work all day,

soon you'll have them full of seed. It's good
to turn over the land in springtime too,
then leave it fallow all summer. True,
that's much more work: the gain is much more food.

You need to sow on soil that's still quite light,
with a memory of summer – before the earth turns cold,
damp and heavy. Fallow land will extend

our lives, and serve our wives and children right,
extending *their* lives too. Seekers of gold,
pray to Zeus, who'll set your dividend.

XXXV

Demeter also. Just as you start to plough,
with the plough-tail in your hand as you play
the switch lightly on the oxen's back, pray
to both deities. Offer the sweat of your brow

as a sacrifice as the oxen strain for your sake
at the yoke-straps. The gods, if your faith is sound,
will bend ripe, heavy corn down to the ground.
Behind you'll need another man, with a rake

to cover the seeds and make more work for finches.
The corn will flourish if the gods agree.
The spiders in your storage bins will quiver

in their webs, which will be swept away. By inches
they'll escape with their lives. You too may be
lucky – given enough to be yourself a giver.

XXXVI

If you start to plough around the shortest day,
your harvest will be scanty – a basketful
perhaps. Neighbours will find you pitiable,
reaping on your knees the pauper's way.

But Zeus' plans are hard for us to tell.
If in the spring, when the cuckoo calls from the oak,
he gives us rains for three whole days, which soak
into the ground and fill up to the level

of an ox's hoof-print, neither more nor less,
then he who ploughs in winter's depths may fare
as well as a more punctual soul. The will

of Zeus makes all the difference: no one can guess
his intentions. Remember this. Take care
to be observant. Farm with a farmer's skill.

XXXVII

Pass right by the smithy where the idlers talk
all day, dodging both the chores and the cold.
Better to work at home with your sleeves rolled
up, indoors and out. Don't let winter walk

off with your livelihood while you sit on a stool
rubbing with scrawny hands your swollen feet –
a sure sign of malnutrition. You'll eat
well enough if you work and don't play the fool.

Hopeful yet idle, many turn to crime.
Gossip is useless – the parliament of dreams,
where lost men keep on losing. No one warns

them of the danger. They're running out of time.
Summer, like winter, isn't all it seems.
Tell your slaves: 'The clock's ticking: build those barns.'

XXXVIII

Lenaeon is the cruellest month, in the grip
of the harsh late winter, when the ox's hide
is pierced by ice. Give this month a wide
berth. Boreas blows deadly winds which whip

across Thrace and lash both woods and sea
into storms. Frost weighs down oaks and firs
to the bountiful earth, and digs its spurs
into the flanks of life, mercilessly.

The forest groans. Animals shiver, and fold
their tails under their genitals – even those
blessed with fur coats. The North Wind slices through

the shaggiest pelts – all succumb to the cold,
except the sheep's fleece. Only a sheep can doze
through such a day, when human flesh turns blue.

XXXIX

This harsh wind curves an old man like a wheel,
but leaves untouched the fragrant girl who stays
by her mother's side indoors, innocent of the ways
of Aphrodite – more bud than flower still.

Just washed, she anoints with oil her tender skin
and then lies down for an afternoon sleep
in an alcove. Far away, in a jumbled heap
of legs, the octopus in its foreign

realm takes a bite of one foot so as not to starve
in its heartless, dismal home, for the sun
has taken its lantern to Africa: it can't see

its prey. Elsewhere, dreaming of a sheltering cave
or thicket, forest creatures on the run,
panicked by snow, are desperate for sanctuary.

XL

Find your own shelter too, in a fleecy cloak
reaching down to your ankles, woven thick,
so your body's hairs lie still and don't stick
out with a shudder. Your blood's heat will stoke

your private furnace. Wear boots of ox hide,
felt-lined, and when the worst of the weather
comes, stitch the skins of new-born kids together
with an ox's sinew and wear them when you ride

or walk in the rain as a cloak on your back
to keep you dry. Don a felt cap as well,
a fitted one that's snug around your ears.

Rain looks in the sky for the slightest crack
to fling itself through. But, given the right apparel,
we can all defend ourselves against its spears.

XLI

Look to your health. Boreas chills the dawn,
and over the shivering land spreads a veil of mist,
drawn from the river, squeezed from the fist
of winter. By evening, from the wind-torn

skies, merciless rain will often tumble down,
sometimes with storms as the clouds turn inky-black
and thicken, with a flash and a loud crack
of thunder. Everyone fears their farm might drown.

Outwit Boreas. Finish your work and be sure
to get home ahead of him, staying safe and dry.
Lenaeon's a difficult month for man and beast.

Give less food to each ox; to yourself, more.
The long nights help – though the unlucky die.
Conserve your pantry till the season lets you feast.

XLII

Once Zeus has given us sixty wintry days
after the solstice, Arcturus, following
the Great Bear, rises again at dusk, glowing
bright in the darkening sky as it strays

from Oceanus, the starry belt that confines
the Earth. Then the swallow from her darkness flies,
telling of spring in plaintive assemblies.
Forestall her: before she visits, prune your vines.

Soon, when the snail, fleeing the Pleiades,
climbs up the plant-stem, sharpen your scythes and rouse
your slaves. Be quicker than he is. When the corn

ripens, harvest. Don't laze in the shade of trees.
Be on the road by sunrise: let others drowse.
Esteem your fellow worker – namely, dawn.

XLIII

Beware the month the golden thistle flowers,
and perched inside its tree the cicada sings
its endless anthem from underneath its wings.
Goats are fattest, wine has the headiest powers,

women are at their most lascivious –
and men at this time are at their weakest,
their joints like jelly, jelly-like all their zest,
their brains parched by the dog-star, Sirius.

To escape the sun, sit in a rock's shadow.
Lunch on Thracian wine and milky bread. Dine
on cheese from dehydrated goats, with the meat

of new-born kids and a forest-grazing cow.
Mix three parts spring water with one part wine.
Turn your face to Zephyrus to dodge the heat.

XLIV

When Orion appears, tell your slaves to winnow
Demeter's sacred grain on a well-aired yard
with a well-rolled threshing floor. It isn't hard
to decant the lot into storage jars, so you know

how much you have. Then wheel the jars inside.
Turn out your hired man, and instead install
a loyal serving girl who'll cater for all
your needs in the home – someone who isn't tied

to a child who'd get under your feet all the time.
Acquire an excitable dog, and feed him well
to guard against thieves who'll strike out of the blue.

To keep your mules and oxen in their prime,
bring them plenty of hay and litter. Tell
your slaves to relax. Unyoke your oxen too.

XLV

When Orion and the dog-star Sirius blaze
in the open sky, and Arcturus lights his wick
at sunrise, that's the time, Perses, to pick
your grapes, and take them home, and for ten days

spread them all out on the ground in the sun
and for another five days raise a canopy
over them for shade, slung from tree to tree,
and on the sixteenth day pour into great stone

storage jars this blessing from Dionysus,
good god of wine who cheers the downcast heart.
When the Pleiades and the Hyades disappear,

and Orion sinks too, it's time to leave the house
in the care of your trusty servant girl and start
to plough. So ends, thank Zeus, another year.

XLVI

Even if the sailor's joy has filled your heart,
when Orion chases the Pleiades into the waves
and furious storms take men to watery graves,
bring home your boat and take a landsman's part.

Pull your craft up onto the shore. Devise
a cradle of close-packed stones to keep
it safe from gales. And to let floodwater seep
away, remove the bilge-plug: otherwise

Zeus with his rains will rot the timbers through.
Fold up the sails, ensuring their angles match.
Stow all your gear in the house: order it well.

Hang your rudder over smoke – all sailors do.
Then dream of the ocean foam. Longingly watch
from the shore till again you embrace the swell.

XLVII

When the time's right for sailing, take your boat
down to the shore and load it with cargo
you can sell to strangers overseas to show
a profit. Such prospects might seem remote

to you, brother Perses, but after all
it's what our father did for want of scope
on land. Seafaring was his only hope
and years ago brought him here, as you'll recall,

from Aeolian Cyme, compelled by Zeus
to escape bleak poverty in a black ship.
He settled in a village, Ascra, near

Helicon – a wretched place of little use
to humankind, desperate in winter's grip
and miserable at any time of year.

XLVIII

But Perses, let's return to you. Bear in mind
that every kind of work has its own season,
seafaring especially. Heap praise upon
a small boat, but be sure you always find

a large one for your cargo. The more you take,
the more you'll sell — so long as the weather
holds and storms don't leave you altogether
bankrupt, for Zeus can break as well as make

a life. If you're resolved to end misery —
the debt, the hunger — by taking up commerce,
clear your dumb brain for the wisdom I'll dispense.

I'll teach you to take the measure of the sea.
I've no first-hand knowledge to impart, but verse,
all poets agree, transcends experience.

XLIX

Myself, I've never — yet — sailed the open sea,
except from Aulis where the Achaeans,
dreaming of the fair women of Troy, once
mustered a great host, and cast off eagerly.

But I sailed only to Chalcis, just off the coast,
for the funeral games of Amphidamas
whose sons had established prizes for verse
and other skills. Forgive me if I boast:

I carried off the tripod in those games,
dedicating it to the Heliconian Muses
who'd taught me to sing so clear and true.

I joined the rollcall of illustrious names,
proud of my skills, proud of my poet's bruises.
This is all I've done at sea, I confess to you.

L

The season for sailing starts again fifty days
after the solstice, in the cool respite
after the angry sun has lost its bite.
From the shelter of river-mouths and bays

mariners safely venture. You can be sure
your boat won't end up as a sunken wreck,
nor your crew be swept by a wave off the deck
to be lost in a mountainous ocean – or

if not quite sure, then confident at least,
so long as Poseidon, shaker of land and sea,
and Zeus, king of immortals, are satisfied

with calm, curbing their tendency to feast
on destruction. For these are the gods of destiny,
who make things happen, good or bad – they decide.

LI

This is the time when various breezes blow,
all easy to assess, and the sea lies flat.
Now you can put to sea in the knowledge that
all should be well. Get busy. Load your cargo.

Set sail, but hurry back. Don't take your ease,
awaiting the new wine or the autumn rains.
Don't be caught by the season of hurricanes,
when Notus, the South Wind, churns up tall seas.

Some traders choose instead to sail in spring
when the leaves at the top of a fig tree
are as large as the footprints of a crow.

This is a risky venture – not something
I'd recommend. The chance is seized too hastily:
your voyage may end in grief for all you know.

LII

Yet many take this course – you can see why.
They accept the risk when money is the key
to survival. And yet to be lost at sea,
spluttering for breath – that's a terrible way to die.

I'm serious: take heed of my advice.
This is practical wisdom, which could save
your life. Try to be wise as well as brave.
To sail in spring is to gamble with dangerous dice.

Don't put all your wealth in ships in any case.
You'll break the axle if you overload the cart.
To spread the risk, keep some of your goods in store

for future trips. The waves are an awful place
for all your hopes to perish in your heart,
along with all your goods, as you pace the shore.

LIII

Have good regard for measure in all you do.
Whatever the situation, act with reason.
Bring a wife to your house in good season
when you're about thirty, no more than a few

years more or less: this is the time to wed.
Choose a wife who's four years past puberty
and a virgin, so you have the security
of knowing that she'll learn from you in bed.

Marry a girl who lives not far away
after scouring all round your neighbourhood,
or folk might chuckle at your choice of bride.

A good wife is a treasure, most would say,
while a bad wife can break even a good,
strong man, happier in the arms of suicide.

LIV

Beware of the gods, who'll punish every wrong.
Don't treat a friend the way you treated me,
your brother: deal with him honourably.
Don't start a quarrel or twist him round your tongue

with lies. But if he insults you first or fights
against your interest or tries to deceive you,
pay him back double, whatever else you do.
Then if he seeks to put the wrong to rights

and shows regret, welcome him to your love
again, once the mist of suspicion clears.
The man who casts off friendship without a trace

of care or conscience, like slipping off a glove,
will never be well thought of by his peers.
Be as open in your thoughts as in your face.

LV

Avoid acquiring for yourself a name
for being too mean with your welcome, or too free.
Measure in all things. Don't choose your company
from the *hoi polloi*, nor spin tales to defame

the nobility. And don't reproach the poor
for a fate wished on them by the immortal gods
as desperately they struggle against the odds.
Think of your tongue as the key to a store

where gold and dross are mixed. Take only gold
and then give it away, with nonchalance.
Offering dross will bring you more dross in return.

And don't be moody, petulant or cold
with guests at dinner – the food's no great expense,
and companionship's too fine a thing to spurn.

LVI

Never pour a libation of wine at dawn to Zeus,
or any god, with unwashed hands, or they
just won't listen: your prayers will drain away.
On the subject of wine and dawn, there's an abuse

I should warn you against: don't face the sun
when you urinate. Piss after the sun has set
or before it rises. Even then, never forget
that the night belongs to the blessed gods, and none

of them wants to see you with your tackle out.
Don't piss in the road, even well towards one side.
The god-fearing man slinks to a private place –

a shady wall perhaps, or a rain-spout
that will drown the noise. The rule is: hide.
If you *must* piss in public, crouch, and mask your face.

LVII

Indoors, don't lie down naked by the fire
after lovemaking, besmirched with sperm and sweat –
the gods don't want to see this. Also, you'll regret
the deed if you conceive a child after

a funeral – much better after a solemn ceremony
in honour of the immortals. And to return
to my earlier point, be sure not to earn
the wrath of the gods by pissing irreverently

in a river or fountain – and don't defecate,
that's no better. Before you wade through a stream
or river, pray. Admire the purity

of the water, marvel at its fluid state –
tangible, yet evanescent as a dream,
like hopes of joy in the shadow of blasphemy.

LVIII

Don't clip your nails during the sacred feast.
And never, when drinking, leave the ladle
in the mixing-bowl, or you'll bring some wrathful
retribution on your head – gut-ache at least.

Don't leave a house unfinished if you begin
to build one, or you'll find the ominous crow
will settle there and croak to let you know
bad luck is coming. Pre-empt its baleful din.

Many such commandments you must take
to heart, or be punished. Another is, don't eat
from or wash in an unblessed pot. And you

mustn't sit a baby boy on a tomb: it will make
him unmanly. Similarly, don't be so effete
as to wash in a woman's bathwater – that's taboo.

LIX

And when you come across a stranger's sacrifice,
smouldering away, and it's different from what *you*'d do,
don't snipe – the gods dislike such arrogance too.
If you scoff at the unknown you'll pay the price.

I've described some of the ways to act – or not to.
But avoid the useless, poisonous *talk* of men.
Talk is light, and easy to float, but when
it's airborne, flown by its garrulous crew,

it can be hard to bring back down to earth.
We're powerless to affect its wayward flight,
willed by the multitude – as if it's shod

in wingèd sandals, carrying news of the birth
of monsters to unsettle us. Talk is quite
pervasive – and ineradicable, like a god.

LX

Acquaint yourself with the calendar Zeus designed.
Brief your slaves on each day's personality.
The thirtieth of the month is best to oversee
work and deal out food – keep this in mind

if you want to be masterful. Some days excel.
The first, fourth and seventh have special worth,
the seventh being the day Leto gave birth
to Apollo with his golden sword, as the poets tell.

This day's revered. Others are holy as well,
especially the eighth and ninth. Two further days
in the waxing moon, the eleventh and twelfth, suit

manual labour: opt for one when you fell
trees to clear land for animals to graze,
build a barn, shear sheep, or harvest grain or fruit.

LXI

The twelfth, in fact, is more auspicious by far
than the eleventh. It's then the high-flying
spider spins its web in the air, defying
gravity, and the canny ant collects its store.

This is the time a woman should dust off
her loom and start her weaving. The following
day, the thirteenth, is unsuitable for sowing,
but for bedding in plants it's good enough.

The sixth day of the waning moon's the wrong time
for any kind of plants, but favourable
for the birth of a baby boy. Well fed,

he'll fend off illness and enjoy his prime.
Yet this same day, for a woman, is full
of grief – a bad day to be born or wed.

LXII

Nor is the sixth day of the waxing moon
promising for a baby girl to be born,
but it's a fine day for grabbing a ram by the horn
and castrating it – and you'll find good fortune

too if you perform this delicate operation
on a kid, or choose this day to enclose
your flocks with a fence – a good farmer knows
what to do when, and with what expectation.

A man born on this day will thrive as a rule –
though he'll be fond of mockery and lies
and devious whispers. The eighth day's good to castrate

a boar or a bellowing bull, the twelfth a mule.
If you want to know if a boy will turn out wise,
ask when was he born: the twentieth's the best date.

LXIII

The tenth's an auspicious day for a boy
to take his first gulp of fresh Grecian air,
while the fourth of the waxing moon bodes fair
for a girl, whom the gods may bless with joy.

On this day lay your hands upon your sheep
to tame them – likewise train your oxen,
your mules and your dog. The fourth will often
bring heartbreaking worry and steal your sleep –

in both waxing and waning moons. You may
bring home a bride then, but only if you find
a favourable omen in a pattern of bird

flight. Beware of the terrible fifth day –
when the Furies helped Strife to bear the maligned
Horcus, who punishes those who break their word.

LXIV

On the waning seventh, winnow the holy grain,
gift of Demeter. Or if you're a carpenter,
cut boards for a bed that fits together
well, or for a boat. If the latter, refrain

from building it till the fourth, boatbuilders say.
Then there's the waning ninth, which tends to bring
misfortune at first, then towards evening
improves. By contrast the waxing ninth is a day

uniformly benign, and for the delivery
of a boy or girl the perfect time. Few know
that the twenty-seventh is best to open

a cask and let the wine or grain run free,
or skilfully place a yoke, easy and slow,
on the neck of a swift-footed horse – or yoke your oxen.

LXV

This is a fine day too if you need to pull
a swift boat down to the sea. A storage jar
is best broached on the waning fourth – by far
the holiest day, for sure. And it's shameful

how few people know the twenty-first
is the best of all at dawn but then swings round
from good to bad and on the rebound
slaps you hard: towards evening it's the worst!

Such days are a tainted blessing. Others make
no sense at all – for one of these random days
might give like a mother or grab like a mother-in-law.

Happy are those who know all this, and take
care not to upset the gods, but sing their praise,
work hard, and try to be just. Who can do more?

Notes

Notes on the Poems

'Most' and 'Wender' refer to the English translations by Glenn W. Most and Dorothea Wender. 'Graves' refers to Robert Graves, *The Greek Myths*. All three sources are cited in full on p. 6 of this book. Numbers in brackets not prefixed by 'line(s)' refer to lines of the Greek original (in the Most edition). 'Line(s)' indicates a reference to the sonnets themselves.

Theogony

Invocation Helicon (line 4), a mountain in Boeotia, is celebrated as the favourite haunt of the nine Muses. Hesiod describes the Muses washing themselves in one of three springs there (Permessus, Hippocrene or Olmeius) before dancing and singing around the altar of their father Zeus.

I p. 26 Chaos is rendered by Most as 'Chasm' – a gap or opening rather than a 'cosmic brew' (line 2). Tartarus (line 9) is a hellish place of punishment far below the Underworld. The reference to the falling anvil is borrowed from later in the *Theogony* (722–3).

III p. 27 The idea of Oceanus as a stream girdling Earth occurs, more than once, in Homer; most notably, it lies behind his description in the *Iliad* of Achilles' shield with its all-enclosing border (xviii, 607–9). 'Much-kissed' (line 13) is my own elaboration: Hesiod describes Thetys simply as 'lovely'.

IV p. 28 Pointing out that *Cyclops* means 'ring-eyed', Graves (3.2) suggests the Cyclopes probably had concentric rings tattooed on their foreheads in honour of the sun: hence 'tattooed faces' (line 5). Hesiod doesn't mention the Cyclopes' skill in building walls but Graves does (3b). They were said to have built the 'Cyclopean' fortifications at Tiryns and Mycenae in the Peloponnese.

hardly the Three Graces (line 8): my own joke, of course (I was thinking of the famous neo-classical sculpture by Canova). Hesiod tells of the birth of the Graces, or Charites, later in the *Theogony*, in the long passage on the Olympian descendants; and in the *Works and Days* he has them adorning the newly created Pandora with jewellery (73–4), though I omit this reference in my version (sonnet V).

(their names are unimportant). (line 14): Hesiod does give the names of

the three fifty-headed, hundred-armed sons of Earth: Cottus, Briareus and Gyges.

V p. 29   *adamant* (line 10): a mythical metal, harder than any other known substance. Perseus used a sickle of adamant to decapitate the Gorgon Medusa (Graves 73g).

VII p. 30   *Longing for love he lay across the land, / fully extended.* (lines 1–2): Wender has 'Longing for love, he lay around the Earth, / Spreading out fully.' Her first five words seemed unimprovably right.

VIII   p. 31   Hesiod has grass, not flowers, growing beneath Aphrodite's feet. He doesn't mention the doves, but see Graves (11b).

IX p. 31   My list of Night's offspring (lines 2–4) omits Ker (a spirit of death), the Fates, Nemesis, Deceit, Fondness, Old Age and Strife. In turn Strife gives birth to Toil, Forgetfulness and other ills. My octave stands in for many densely compacted couplings occupying almost 230 lines of the original (226–452). Some of Hesiod's lines comprise just three or four alien proper names, eg 'Doto and Proto and Pherusa and Dynamene'. The 'various parents' include Pontus and his sons Nereus and Thaumus. The offspring include monsters, such as the Gorgons, Cerberus and Hydra; the fifty Nereids; and many rivers, notably the Nile and the Styx. In this long passage Hesiod also provides extra-condensed summaries of some of the labours of Heracles. The most significant of the 'life-givers' (line 8) is Hecate, who bestows happiness on any mortal who invokes her in the performance of sacrificial rites.

XIII p. 34   In moving straight to the 'grim world war' (line 1) I skip a long passage that begins with more couplings, resulting in the births of Atlas, Menoetius, Prometheus and Epimetheus (507–634). Hesiod tells of the punishments Zeus chooses for these wicked sons of Iapetus, concluding in Prometheus being chained to a pillar and visited each day by an eagle which devours his self-renewing liver. He describes the defeat of the eagle by Heracles and, finally, Prometheus' original transgression, which had been to show mankind how to deprive Zeus of his fair share of a sacrificial ox. I use this latter detail in my version of the *Works and Days* to amplify and clarify the account of the Prometheus story given there (IV).

XIV p. 34   My version omits Hesiod's account of the geography and demography of Tartarus and the story of Zeus' battle against Typhoeus, the youngest son of Earth. Zeus' wives are named as Metis (Wisdom), Themis (Divine Justice) and Hera. Out of wedlock he coupled with Eurynome, Demeter, Mnemosyne, Leto, Maia, Semele and Alcmene. Hesiod describes the god swallowing Metis to absorb her wisdom, just prior to the birth of Athena; he also tells how Athena grew out of Zeus' own head. Zeus' offspring included the Horae (Seasons), Persephone, the Muses, Apollo, Artemis, Ares, Hermes, Dionysus and Heracles. The idea of him having a 'soft side' (line 9) is a neo-Romantic transgression. I've used nothing from the final passage of the original (963–1022): a farewell to the Olympian gods and a list of children born to goddesses.

Works and Days

I p. 37   *Pierian Muses* (line 1): Pieria, just north of Mount Olympus, was the birthplace of Orpheus and the Muses, and the site of the Pierian Spring – believed to confer knowledge upon anyone who drank from it.

aegis (line 12): Hesiod makes no reference to the 'aegis' in the invocation but does mention it elsewhere in the poem: it's the term given to Zeus' magic cloth or shield. The sight of Zeus shaking storms out of his aegis was said to induce panic in the beholder. The goddess Athena also had one.

II p. 37   *Strife is no only child: there are two of them.* (line 1): this may be a conscious revision of a mention in the *Theogony*, where Strife is identified as the offspring of Night (225).

It's beggar against beggar, bard against bard. (line 14): I've omitted potters and builders and I've inserted a 'prize cow'; but the beggars and poets are in the original.

III p. 38   *Demeter's gift* (line 6): Demeter is the goddess of grain and fertility.

IV p. 38   *We'd tried to fool him when / an ox was apportioned between gods and men, / and Zeus was offered only bones to boil.* (lines 6–8): I've borrowed this background detail from the *Theogony* (see my note on sonnet XIII above).

V p. 39   According to Hesiod, Hermes furnished Pandora with a dog's mind and a thief's character but I refer, more mildly, to her slyness. Athena *gave* her a girdle and ornaments: my 'loaned' (line 9) makes the goddess sound more human, I hope. I omit Hesiod's reference to Pallas Athena adorning the girl with jewellery donated by the Graces and Persuasion.

this was ironic. (line 14): the irony is definitely there in the Hesiod, but less heavy-handedly so: '[The gods] had given her a gift – a woe for men who live on bread' (Most 81–82).

VII p. 40   Most points out that the common translation 'Hope' (line 4) is not quite faithful to the original: he opts instead for 'Anticipation'.

VIII p. 41   *Snake and scorpion bared no sting.* (line 7): there's no such detail in Hesiod.

possibly in an earthquake or a flood (line 11): Hesiod says merely that 'the earth covered up this race' (Most 121), a formula he applies also to the races of silver and bronze.

and joy where music's heard, (line 13): this is derived from Graves (5b): 'their spirits survive as genii of happy music retreats'.

IX p. 42   *shorter* (line 2) is guesswork. Hesiod is more generous to this race in the end than I am: 'but all the same honour attends upon these as well' (Most 142).

X p. 42   Hesiod has the additional detail that the bronze race worked in bronze: 'there was not any black iron' (Most 151).

XI p. 43   *some, seeking the flocks of Oedipus* (line 8): the attack on Thebes was conducted by the supporters of Polyneices, one of the twin sons of Oedipus by his mother Jocasta. He was attemping to usurp Eteocles, his brother, as ruler of the city – they'd been declared co-rulers after Oedipus' banishment.

XII p. 44   *They'll let whole towns fall into disrepair.* (line 12): Hesiod has the men of this race *destroying* each other's towns.

Wretched and godless, (line 13): my justification for mentioning godlessness is a brief reference in Hesiod: 'cruel men, who do not know the gods' retribution!' (Most 186).

they'll worship the moon… / or nothing. Athens will sink with the rise of Rome. (lines 13–14): none of this is in Hesiod; and the reference to Rome, of course, is wildly anachronistic.

XIV p. 45   Hesiod directs his little fable to 'kings who themselves too have understanding' (Most 202), but soon forgets about the kings he's supposed to be addressing.

clear as the wine-dark sea. (line 1): not in the Hesiod.

XV p. 46   Most has 'Outrageousness' rather than Greed (line 1), while Wender speaks of 'pride'. I may have distorted the original but Greed seems to me more relevant to Perses' transgressions against the poet and a more appropriate quality to place in opposition to Justice.

She arrests the mob, setting the informant free. (line 14): this has no basis in Hesiod.

XVII p. 47   I've expanded Hesiod's description of the effects of wickedness to include vagueness in doctors and the destruction of wells. Violence against armies, walls and ships is all there in the original.

XIX p. 48   Hesiod praying to Zeus to make him innocent of the urge for self-preservation (line 7) stretches a small, unclear point in the original.

XXVII p. 54   The Pleiades (line 2), also known as the Seven Sisters, a star-cluster within the constellation of Taurus, rises in the first half of May and sets in late October or early November. On a clear night it's easily located by following the line of Orion's belt up to the right.

For forty nights these high-born girls lie low; (line 4): Hesiod refers to 'the Atlas-born girls'.

XXIX p. 55   I made up the idea of working indoors in stormy weather (line 11). Later the farmer is advised to 'plough away… whether it's dry or wet, / all season long' (sonnet XXXIV) – not a contradiction, as a storm would surely have made ploughing impossible.

XXX p. 56   *When… Sirius takes a smaller share of day, / a larger share of night* (lines 1–5): that is, late September or early October.

A 'ten-palm cart' (line 14) would have been about 2 feet 6 inches wide.

'Three span' is about 2 feet 3 inches.

XXXI p. 56   *one of Athena's men* (line 6): that is, a carpenter.

XXXIII p. 58   *Every year when you hear the voice of cranes* (line 1): having bred in the wetlands of Asia, the migrating cranes arrive to winter in southern Europe in late October or early November.

XXXVII p. 60   *a sure sign of malnutrition.* (line 7): Most explains this in a footnote (to 497), since Hesiod gives the symptom but not the diagnosis.

'The clock's ticking: build those barns.' (line 14): this echoes Wender's reading of the Greek, but Most offers a different interpretation: 'Make huts for yourselves' (503).

XXXVIII p. 61   Lenaeon (line 1) is the second half of January and the beginning of February. Boreas (line 4) is the North Wind.

XLII p. 64   Arcturus (line 2), the second brightest star in the northern sky (after Sirius), rises in the second half of February. The snail could be described as fleeing the Pleiades after its rising in the first half of May.

XLIII p. 64   The golden thistle (line 1), which belongs to the genus *Scolymus*, flowers in July. Zephyrus (line 14) is the West Wind, bringer of summer breezes.

XLIV p. 65   *When Orion appears,* (line 1): Most identifies the time precisely as 20 June; Wender suggests July.

XLV p. 66   *When Orion and the dog-star Sirius blaze / in the open sky, and Arcturus lights his wick / at sunrise* (lines 1–3): that is, mid-September.

When the Pleiades and the Hyades disappear, / and Orion sinks too, (lines 11–12): that is, October.

it's time to leave the house / in the care of your trusty servant girl and start / to plough. (lines 12–14): I've added the reference to the servant girl. In sonnet XLIV we learn that she's brought into the household after the hired man has been turned out in late June (Most) or July (Wender). I'm uncertain whether this is the woman mentioned in sonnet XXIX, where the farmer is urged to find 'someone who can follow him with the oxen' (Most 406) as well as set up the household.

XLVI p. 66   *when Orion chases the Pleiades into the waves* (line 2): that is, November.

XLVII p. 67   *Aeolian Cyme* (line 9): Cyme was the largest of twelve cities in Aeolia (or Aeolis), a western and north-western region of Asia Minor which includes several offshore islands, notably Lesbos. All these cities were on the coast of what is now Turkey.

XLVIII p. 68   *but verse, / all poets agree, transcends experience.* (lines 13–14): this is an interpolation – anachronistic, of course.

XLIX p. 68   Aulis (line 2) is the port in Boeotia, in north-central Greece, from which the Greek fleet set out for Troy at the outset of the Trojan War. Chalcis, the main town on the island of Euboea, is separated from Aulis by a narrow strait. Amphidamas was a nobleman of Chalcis. Achaeans is one of the collective names used for the Greeks in Homer's *Iliad* and *Odyssey*.

proud of my poet's bruises. (line 13): another interpolation in the same spirit as sonnet XLVIII, lines 13–14 (see above).

L p. 69   *fifty days / after the solstice* (lines 1–2): Most interprets the safe period for sailing as stretching from 21 June until well into August but I've followed Wender, who tells us that it isn't safe to sail *until* the fifty days have elapsed.

LIII p. 71   *happier in the arms of suicide.* (line 14): Hesiod has the wife singeing her husband (or 'roasting him alive' as Wender puts it) without a torch and condemning him to a raw old age.

LVI p. 73   Hesiod refers to 'the wall of a well-fenced courtyard' (Most 732) but doesn't mention the rain-spout to drown the noise (lines 12–13). He does talk about crouching to urinate. 'Mask your face' (line 14) is pure invention on my part.

LIX p. 75   Hesiod has only five lines on talk, which I've expanded, adding the 'wingèd sandals' and 'news of the birth of monsters' (lines 12–13).

LX p. 76   *Leto gave birth / to Apollo* (lines 7–8): the father was Zeus. Leto was the daughter of the Titans Coeus and Phoebe.

waxing moon, (line 11): Hesiod's month was divided into two halves: the waxing moon and the waning moon. Given a thirty-day month, the 'sixth day of the waning moon', for example, would be the 21st. However, Hesiod sometimes omits the waxing/waning prefix and refers to days of the month exactly as we would.

Sample Prose Translations

Readers interested in knowing what kinds of liberties I have taken with Hesiod's meaning are invited to make comparisons with the following literal prose translations, corresponding to sonnets V and X of my *Theogony* and sonnets X, XX, XXX, XL, L and LX of my *Works and Days*. The translations are by Hugh G. Evelyn-White (1914) and can be found in full at www.sacred-texts.com/cla/hesiod/theogony.htm and www.sacred-texts.com/cla/hesiod/works.htm

Theogony

Sonnet V / *from* 154*ff*
For of all the children that were born of Earth and Heaven, these

were the most terrible, and they were hated by their own father from the first.

And he used to hide them all away in a secret place of Earth so soon as each was born, and would not suffer them to come up into the light: and Heaven rejoiced in his evil doing. But vast Earth groaned within, being straitened, and she made the element of grey flint and shaped a great sickle, and told her plan to her dear sons. And she spoke, cheering them, while she was vexed in her dear heart:

'My children, gotten of a sinful father, if you will obey me, we should punish the vile outrage of your father; for he first thought of doing shameful things.'

Sonnet X / *from 459ff*

These great Cronos swallowed as each came forth from the womb to his mother's knees with this intent, that no other of the proud sons of Heaven should hold the kingly office amongst the deathless gods. For he learned from Earth and starry Heaven that he was destined to be overcome by his own son, strong though he was, through the contriving of great Zeus. Therefore he kept no blind outlook, but watched and swallowed down his children: and unceasing grief seized Rhea.

Works and Days

Sonnet X / *from 143ff*

... Zeus the Father made a third generation of mortal men, a brazen race, sprung from ash-trees; and it was in no way equal to the silver age, but was terrible and strong. They loved the lamentable works of Ares and deeds of violence; they ate no bread, but were hard of heart like adamant, fearful men. Great was their strength and unconquerable the arms which grew from their shoulders on their strong limbs. Their armour was of bronze, and their houses of bronze, and of bronze were their implements: there was no black iron. These were destroyed by their own hands and passed to the dank house of chill Hades, and left no name: terrible though they were, black Death seized them, and they left the bright light of the sun.

Sonnet XX / *from 286ff*

To you, foolish Perses, I will speak good sense. Badness can be got easily and in shoals: the road to her is smooth, and she lives very near us. But between us and Goodness the gods have placed the sweat of our brows: long and steep is the path that leads to her, and it is rough at the first; but when a man has reached the top, then is she easy to reach, though before that she was hard.

That man is altogether best who considers all things himself and marks what will be better afterwards and at the end; and he, again, is good who listens to a good adviser; but whoever neither thinks for himself nor keeps in mind what another tells him, he is an unprofitable man.

Sonnet XXX / *from 414ff*

When the piercing power and sultry heat of the sun abate, and almighty Zeus sends the autumn rains, and men's flesh comes to feel far easier, – for then the star Sirius passes over the heads of men, who are born to misery, only a little while by day and takes greater share of night, – then, when it showers its leaves to the ground and stops sprouting, the wood you cut with your axe is least liable to worm. Then remember to hew your timber: it is the season for that work. Cut a mortar three feet wide and a pestle three cubits long, and an axle of seven feet, for it will do very well so; but if you make it eight feet long, you can cut a beetle from it as well. Cut a felloe three spans across for a waggon of ten palms' width.

Sonnet XL / *from 536ff*

Then put on, as I bid you, a soft coat and a tunic to the feet to shield your body, – and you should weave thick woof on thin warp. In this clothe yourself so that your hair may keep still and not bristle and stand upon end all over your body.

Lace on your feet close-fitting boots of the hide of a slaughtered ox, thickly lined with felt inside. And when the season of frost comes on, stitch together skins of firstling kids with ox-sinew, to put over your back and to keep off the rain. On your head above wear a shaped cap of felt to keep your ears from getting wet...

Sonnet L / *from 663ff*

Fifty days after the solstice, when the season of wearisome heat is come to an end, is the right time for me to go sailing. Then you will not wreck your ship, nor will the sea destroy the sailors, unless Poseidon the Earth-Shaker be set upon it, or Zeus, the king of the deathless gods, wish to slay them; for the issues of good and evil alike are with them.

Sonnet LX / *from 765ff*

Mark the days which come from Zeus, duly telling your slaves of them, and that the thirtieth day of the month is best for one to look over the work and to deal out supplies.

For these are days which come from Zeus the all-wise, when men discern aright.

To begin with, the first, the fourth, and the seventh – on which Leto bare Apollo with the blade of gold – each is a holy day. The eighth and the ninth, two days at least of the waxing month, are specially good for the works of man. Also the eleventh and twelfth are both excellent, alike for shearing sheep and for reaping the kindly fruits...

Selected titles from the Oxford*Poets* list

Oxford*Poets*, an imprint of Carcanet Press, celebrates the vitality and diversity of contemporary poetry in English.

Joseph Brodsky *Collected Poems In English*
For Brodsky, to be a poet was an absolute, a total necessity...scintillating deployment of language, and always tangential or odd ways of interpreting ideas, events or other literature. John Kinsella, OBSERVER

Carmen Bugan *Crossing the Carpathians*
To say these poems are beautiful is to risk underselling them. It is the specific nature of their beauty that matters, compounded as it is of dark experience, hope, magic, delight, generosity and love of language. George Szirtes

Greg Delanty *Collected Poems 1986–2006*
The fundamental tension that spurs Delanty's poetry crosses the domestic with the wayward, the retrospective with the prospective, and the result is a body of work that has grown steadily from book to book in depth, invention, and ambition. AGENDA

Jane Draycott *The Night Tree*
Hers is a scrupulous intelligence...Her searching curiosity and wonderful assurance make her an impeccable and central poetic intelligence. Penelope Shuttle, MANHATTAN REVIEW

Sasha Dugdale *The Estate*
Dugdale creates a spare, mythical tone that fits itself perfectly to the elemental Russian landscape in which much of her collection is set. GUARDIAN

Rebecca Elson *A Responsibility to Awe*
This is a wise and haunting volume, which I can't recommend too warmly. Boyd Tonkin, INDEPENDENT

Nigel Forde *A Map of the Territory*
Nigel Forde is a natural poet... It's obvious that both experience and thought make their impact on him in a rich mixture of imagery, rhythm and structure that enables them to be carried to us effortlessly. Arnold Wesker

Marilyn Hacker *Essays on Departure*
Everything is thrilling and true, fast and witty, deep and wise; her vitality is the pulse of life itself Derek Mahon

Anthony Hecht *Flight Among the Tombs*
Anthony Hecht's majestic development into a great poet has progressed across half-a-century. Flight Among the Tombs is his poignant and ironic masterpiece. Harold Bloom

Tim Kendall *Strange Land*
An intense and demanding collection. Its metaphysical honesty and its relevance demand our concentration. CHURCH TIMES

Jenny Lewis *Fathom*
The 'fathom' of Jenny Lewis's title resounds through her collection as noun and verb, implying both depth and the reckoning of it…Her poems, in fact, employ many of the techniques of painting, drawing readers in through the gleam of colours so intense and appealing as to be almost edible. GUARDIAN

Lucy Newlyn *Ginnel*
Don't doubt that this is very good poetry indeed…If you require a nostalgic hit of childhood and place, the ingredients which make this collection universal, it is here for you. THE LEEDS GUIDE

Robert Saxton *Manganese*
Intellectually persuasive, tough-minded and strikingly outspoken. This is an extremely well-read, cultured poet…He is also one heck of a craftsman, producing a dexterously sculpted poetry. ORBIS

Peter Scupham *Collected Poems*
He writes wonderfully about places, especially about English places…The sophistication of the technique which underpins every poem becomes clearer and clearer as you read further in this substantial, generous, distinguished volume. Peter Davidson, Books of the Year 2005, READYSTEADYBOOK.COM

Joe Sheerin *Elves in the Wainscotting*
The Irish poet Joe Sheerin's superb second collection… CITY LIFE

Penelope Shuttle *A Leaf Out of his Book*
Some of the poems are very funny…others divertingly offbeat or simply moving…there is a delight in the book as world, the world as book. TIMES LITERARY SUPPLEMENT

Charles Tomlinson *Cracks In the Universe*
Tomlinson is a unique voice in contemporary English poetry, and has been a satellite of excellence for the past 50 years. David Morley, GUARDIAN

Marina Tsvetaeva *Selected Poems*, trans. Elaine Feinstein
Marina Tsvetaeva was the first of the modern Russian poets whose greatness really came clear to me, thanks to these translations. Feinstein has performed the first, indispensable task of a great translator: she has captured a voice. THREEPENNY REVIEW

Chris Wallace-Crabbe *By and Large*
His allies are words, and he uses them with the care of a surgeon and the flair of a conjuror. Peter Porter

---